Flippers and Fins ™

Swimming with Sea Lions

Miriam Coleman

PowerKiDS
press™

New York

Published in 2010 by The Rosen Publishing Group, Inc.
29 East 21st Street, New York, NY 10010

First Edition

Editor: Joanne Randolph
Book Design: Greg Tucker
Photo Researcher: Jessica Gerweck

Photo Credits: Cover © Kevin Schafer/Corbis; pp. 5, 19 Jeff Foott/Getty Images; pp. 7, 13 Shutterstock.com; p. 9 © J&C Sohns/age fotostock; p. 11 © DLILLC/Corbis; p. 15 © Theo Allofs/Corbis; p. 17 Sue Flood/Getty Images; p. 21 © Paul Souders/Corbis.

Library of Congress Cataloging-in-Publication Data

Coleman, Miriam.
   Swimming with sea lions / Miriam Coleman. — 1st ed.
       p. cm. — (Flippers and fins)
   Includes index.
   ISBN 978-1-4042-8095-3 (library binding) — ISBN 978-1-4358-3247-3 (pbk.) —
ISBN 978-1-4358-3248-0 (6-pack)
   1. Sea lions—Juvenile literature. I. Title.
   QL737.P63C65 2010
   599.79'75—dc22
                                                2009006284

Manufactured in the United States of America

Contents

Meet the Sea Lion

On a dock in San Francisco Bay, a pile of sea lions lies asleep in the sun. These fat, **sleek** animals lie around much of the day, rolling on top of each other and barking noisily. With their large eyes and friendly faces, sea lions draw a lot of **admirers**. People come from all over to watch the sea lions on the dock.

Sea lions live mostly along rocky shores in the Pacific Ocean, as well as near the Atlantic coasts of South America and near Australia. The largest sea lions can grow to be 11 feet (3 m) long and can weigh up to 2,200 pounds (998 kg).

This is a California sea lion sitting on the shore of Monterey Bay. There are about 200,000 California sea lions along the Pacific Coast of North America.

Sea Lion or Seal?

Seals and sea lions look very much alike. In fact, sea lions are called eared seals. The ears are one good way to tell sea lions apart from seals. Seals have uncovered openings in their heads. Sea lions have little earflaps.

Sea lions also have different flippers from seals. Sea lions have front flippers that are longer and flatter than seals'. They can use their front and back flippers to walk on land. Seals cannot use their back flippers to walk. Instead, they pull themselves along with their front flippers and powerful stomach muscles. Sea lions are much faster on land than seals are.

Here you can see the sea lion's earflap as well as its beautiful fur. For a long time, sea lions and seals were hunted for their fur, oil, and meat.

Sea Lion Flippers

Sea lions have four flippers. The two flippers in the front, called foreflippers, are wide and shaped like wings. The bones inside the flippers are a lot like a person's finger bones. While most of a sea lion's body is covered with fur, there is no fur on the foreflippers.

The two smaller flippers on the back end of a sea lion are called hind flippers. When a sea lion is on land, it can turn its hind flippers forward in order to walk. Underwater, the sea lion holds its hind flippers out in back and uses them to change direction. The front flippers are used to move the sea lion quickly through the water.

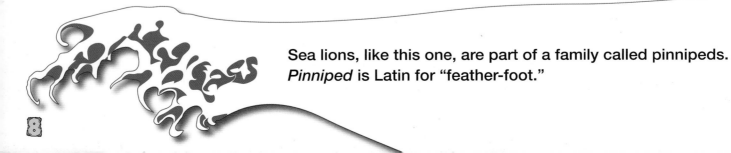

Sea lions, like this one, are part of a family called pinnipeds. *Pinniped* is Latin for "feather-foot."

Built for Speed

Sea lions may look lazy when they are snuggled up together, resting in a pile on the shore. In the water, however, sea lions are built for **speed**. Their bodies are sleek and shaped to cut through the water easily. Sea lions swim forward by moving their foreflippers up and down like wings. They can swim up to 25 miles per hour (40 km/h).

Sea lions are also skilled divers. They find most of their food between 85 and 243 feet (26–74 m) below the surface, but they can dive down almost 900 feet (274 m) if needed. Sea lions can stay underwater without breathing for up to 40 minutes.

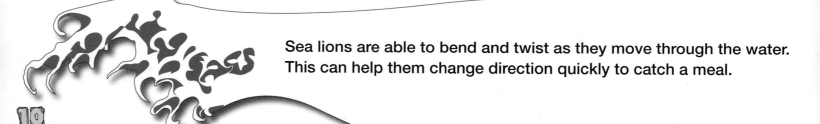

Sea lions are able to bend and twist as they move through the water. This can help them change direction quickly to catch a meal.

Gone Fishing

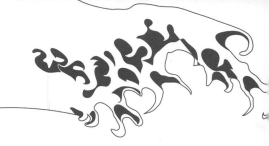

Sea lions do not swim just for fun. They need all their swimming power to catch fast-swimming food from the sea. Sea lions are **predators**, which means that they hunt and eat other animals. They have sharp teeth for catching **prey** and ripping it apart.

Sea lions eat mostly fish, squid, and octopus. Depending on where they live, different types of sea lions might eat different fish, such as salmon, herring, or mackerel. All sea lions will eat whatever they can find, however. Full-grown sea lions can eat up to 40 pounds (18 kg) of food a day!

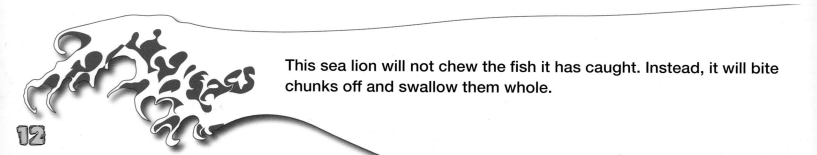

This sea lion will not chew the fish it has caught. Instead, it will bite chunks off and swallow them whole.

Watch Out!

The bodies of sea lions are lined with a thick covering of fat called blubber to keep them warm in the water. All that fat makes sea lions a tasty snack for other predators. Great white sharks and killer whales love to eat sea lions.

Most sea lions can swim fast enough to get away from these predators. Swimming fast and diving deep will generally leave the hunter behind. Sea lions must take extra care on land, where they are slower. If sea lions on land sense a **threat**, they start barking and rush to the sea.

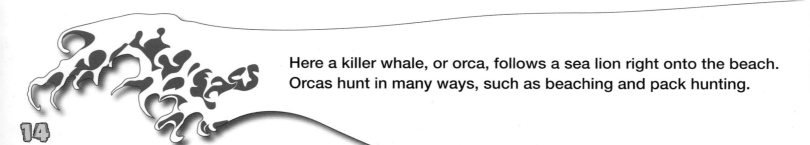

Here a killer whale, or orca, follows a sea lion right onto the beach. Orcas hunt in many ways, such as beaching and pack hunting.

Sea Lion Families

When the season comes for sea lions to **breed**, they come together on islands and beaches. The places where sea lions breed are called rookeries. At the rookeries, the male sea lions, called bulls, fight each other for territory and females. The females are called cows. Sea lion bulls are up to three times larger than cows. They use their large size to fight off other bulls.

Sea lion cows gather around bulls in large groups, called harems. The bull in a harem fathers all the pups, or baby sea lions. He also **protects** the pups and the cows from other bulls. One bull may have as many as 40 cows in his harem.

This is a Steller sea lion colony. Male Steller sea lions do not eat during the breeding season because they need to protect their harem from other bulls.

Sea Lion Pups

Sea lion cows give birth to their pups a year after they breed. They usually have only one pup at a time. The pups are born with brown fur and open eyes. Almost as soon as they are born, the pups can walk and bark. They can even swim, though not very well. Plus sea lion pups do not swim much since they do not have enough blubber when they are born to brave the cold waters where they live.

A few days after giving birth, the mother will start to leave her pup to hunt for food in the sea. After eating her fill, she returns to the rookery to nurse her pup. When a pup is a few weeks old, it will start to play and swim with other pups in the rookery.

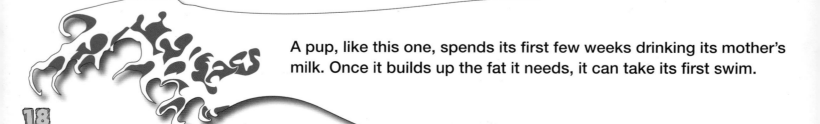

A pup, like this one, spends its first few weeks drinking its mother's milk. Once it builds up the fat it needs, it can take its first swim.

Noisemakers

Sea lions are famous for being noisy. In fact, sea lions are among the noisiest **mammals** on Earth. They bark, growl, roar, trumpet, and grunt. They make sounds under water and on land.

During the breeding season, male sea lions bark all the time to keep other bulls away from their harems. Mother sea lions use a special call to find their pups in a crowd. The mother will make a loud trumpeting noise, and the pup answers with a sound like a lamb's call. The mother and pup **repeat** the sounds until they find each other.

Sea lions have vocal cords in their throats, just as people do. The vocal cords are the parts that let them make so many different sounds.

Smart Sea Lions

Sea lions are **intelligent** animals, and they can easily learn tricks. Zoos and aquariums often put on shows using sea lions. The U.S. Navy has even trained sea lions to find underwater mines. Scientists also study sea lions to find out more about how they think and solve problems.

Although sea lions can help people, people sometimes hurt these animals. **Pollution** that ends up in the ocean can make sea lions sick. For many years, people hunted sea lions for their skin and oil. One kind of sea lion in the Sea of Japan was made **extinct** by hunting. In the United States, it is now unlawful for most people to hunt sea lions.

Glossary

admirers (ud-MY-ur-erz) People who value someone or something a great deal.

breed (BREED) To make babies.

extinct (ek-STINKT) No longer existing.

intelligent (in-TEH-luh-jent) Smart.

mammals (MA-mulz) Warm-blooded animals that have a backbone and hair, breathe air, and feed milk to their young.

pollution (puh-LOO-shun) Humanmade waste that hurts Earth's air, land, or water.

predators (PREH-duh-terz) Animals that kill other animals for food.

prey (PRAY) An animal that is hunted by another animal for food.

protects (pruh-TEKTS) Keeps from harm.

repeat (ree-PEET) To do something again.

sleek (SLEEK) Even and smooth on the outside.

speed (SPEED) How fast something moves.

threat (THRET) A person or thing that may be unsafe.

Index

Web Sites

Due to the changing nature of Internet links, PowerKids Press has developed an online list of Web sites related to the subject of this book. This site is updated regularly. Please use this link to access the list:

www.powerkidslinks.com/ffin/sealion/